Saving Elephants

Contents	Page

written by Suzette Toms

Elephants are the largest and heaviest mammals living on land. They are highly intelligent animals found mostly in Asian and African countries. They live in forests, grasslands, hills and desert-like environments, but never go far from sources of fresh water.

Elephants are a vital species because they impact on the environment in many ways, and their presence or absence affects many other species. Elephants eat enormous quantities of plants, which they do not fully digest, and this partially-digested vegetation is left behind, generating new plant growth. Many rainforest seeds will not germinate until they have passed through an elephant's stomach!

Migrating elephants follow the same paths, making trails that
other animals and people use to travel. With their tusks they
dig wells, creating numerous water sources throughout their
habitat. As elephants move through the environment, they push
plants over like bulldozers, making food accessible to smaller
animals.

All elephants
are in danger of
extinction. The
African elephants are
listed as "vulnerable"
while the Asian
elephant is listed
as "endangered". In
2012, the Sumatran
elephant was
upgraded to "critically
endangered".
Elephant populations
are threatened by
poaching, habitat
loss and conflict with
humans.

Recent studies have shown there are at least three separate species of elephant – the Asian, Savannah and Forest elephants. Although they look very much alike, they have more differences than between the animals of the cat family – the tiger, leopard and lion.

The Savannah and the Forest elephant are found in Africa. The Savannah elephant is the larger of the two, with tusks that curve outwards, whereas Forest elephants are smaller and darker, and their tusks point straight down. Between one quarter and one third of African elephants are Forest elephants.

African elephant populations are spread over 37 countries within the continent. Some populations are endangered, while others are stable or growing. Elephants in Western Africa can be counted in tens or hundreds, and only three countries in this region have more than 1,000 animals. In Southern Africa populations are large and getting bigger, with about 300,000 elephants roaming the region.

Asian elephants are smaller than the African elephant and have smaller ears. They have a single "finger" on the upper lip of the trunk, while African elephants have a second on the lower lip. Some adult male and all female Asian elephants don't grow tusks. Asian elephants are found in at least 13 countries in Southern and South Eastern Asia, including India, Sri Lanka, Vietnam, Thailand, Myanmar, Malaysia, Borneo and Sumatra. The current population of Asian elephants is about 25,000 animals.

Elephants are herbivores, which means they eat only plants. They have such large appetites that more than $2/3$ of an elephant's day is spent feeding – on grasses, tree bark, roots, leaves, stems and fruits. They migrate annually from place to place, allowing the forests and grasslands behind them to regenerate before they return to feed again. They stay close to fresh water sources because they must drink at least once every day.

Farmed crops like bananas, rice and sugar cane are very attractive to elephants. As a result of rising populations and deforestation in Africa and Asia, hungry elephants often come into contact with human settlements. This means they get into trouble with local farmers and growers – they raid crops, trample homes and sometimes even hurt or kill people. Some people strike back and poison or shoot elephants.

Elephants are being pushed into smaller and smaller territories as their migratory paths are blocked. Commercial logging, mining and plantations not only destroy habitat, but also open roads and railway lines that give poachers access to remote elephant populations. Civil wars and violence between countries add to habitat loss.

Poaching is one
of the greatest
threats to elephant
populations world-
wide. In 1989, a
global ban on ivory
helped reduce
the poaching of
elephants. However,
in recent years a
growing demand
for ivory has meant
a huge increase
in poaching. The
capture of wild
elephants for
domestic use is
also a threat to
some populations,
seriously reducing
numbers. Efforts
are being made to
encourage captive
breeding instead of
taking elephants
from the wild.

In 2011, hunting for illegal
ivory was linked to the
death of 2,500 elephants!

There are many worldwide groups trying to save the elephants. They are helping to set up reservations and restore ruined migration paths, so elephants can live and travel safely between food and water sources without disturbing local people.

In some Asian countries squads of trained elephants are used to scare off wild elephants from crops and villages. These squads provide short-term relief to the conflict between people and elephants, and they create support for elephant conservation in poorer communities.

Poaching is illegal worldwide, and in some countries the capture of wild elephants has also been banned. Wildlife guard units carry out anti-poaching patrols; take away snares and animal traps; educate local people on the laws relating to poaching; and help local authorities catch poachers. But there is still so much to be done before elephants are no longer in danger.

If you want to help save the elephants, you can:
- refuse to buy ivory products,
- support conservation groups,
- learn how to help save forests and reduce waste,
- network and spread the word to your friends and family.